COUNTERPOINT WORKBOOK

FOURTH EDITION

Kent Kennan

Professor Emeritus of Music
The University of Texas at Austin

PRENTICE-HALL, INC., Upper Saddle River, New Jersey 07458

© 1999, 1987, 1972, 1959 by Prentice-Hall, Inc.
Pearson Education
Upper Saddle River, New Jersey 07458

Printed in the United States of America

15 16 17 18 V036 14 13 12

ISBN 0-13-081052-5

PRENTICE-HALL INTERNATIONAL (UK) LIMITED, *London*
PRENTICE-HALL OF AUSTRALIA PTY. LIMITED, *Sydney*
PRENTICE-HALL CANADA INC., *Toronto*
PRENTICE-HALL HISPANOAMERICANA, S.A., *Mexico*
PRENTICE-HALL OF INDIA PRIVATE LIMITED, *New Delhi*
PRENTICE-HALL OF JAPAN, INC., *Tokyo*
PRENTICE-HALL OF SOUTHEAST ASIA PTE. LTD., *Singapore*
EDITORA PRENTICE-HALL DO BRASIL, LTDA., *Rio de Janeiro*

Contents

*Kent Kennan, *Counterpoint,* 4th ed. (Upper Saddle River, N.J.: Prentice-Hall, Inc. 1999).

Preface

This *Workbook* is designed to be used in connection with the author's text, *Counterpoint* (fourth edition, 1999), based on eighteenth-century practice. In the preceding Table of Contents, the chapter in the text for which each group of exercises may serve as assignments is indicated. The author did not intend that any one class should do all the exercises; in providing the number of them given here he hoped to meet the needs of different teaching situations and to allow for some variation in the material assigned, from year to year. Additional assignments that do not involve material in the *Workbook* are included in the Suggested Assignments at the ends of chapters in the text.

This edition of the *Workbook* differs from the third edition in a few respects: five "Self Tests" have been moved to the text and reorganized so as to apply to individual chapters; one set of exercises has been deleted, another augmented. The deletions have made it possible to leave the backs of more pages blank, thus reducing the chance that the reverse side of an assigned exercise will contain exercises needed for the next or a later assignment.

It is hoped that the *Workbook* will serve as a helpful supplement both for those students who need to acquire an actual working command of "Baroque-style" counterpoint as part of their background and for those whose study of the subject is intended chiefly to bring about a deeper understanding of the great music that makes up the eighteenth-century contrapuntal tradition.

KENT KENNAN

THE SINGLE LINE; EXERCISES IN ERROR DETECTION

Tell, or write below each example, the error or weakness involved. In the case of Example ⑩ , use the numbers below the staff in referring to specific points. All the examples except numbers ③ and ④ are in C major.

TWO VOICES; 1 : 1; EXERCISES IN ERROR DETECTION

Tell, or write below each example, the error or weakness involved. In the case of Exercise ⑩, use the numbers above it to refer to specific points. Exercises ①-⑨ are in C major, Exercise ⑩ in A-flat major.

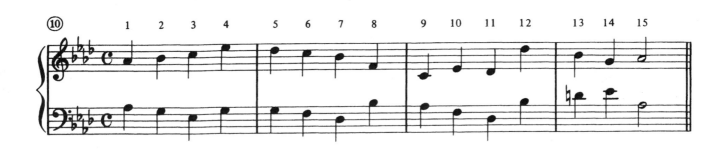

TWO VOICES; 1 : 1, MAJOR, DIATONIC

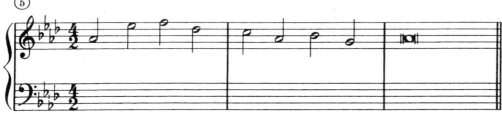

TWO VOICES; 1 : 1, MINOR, DIATONIC

(Raised sixth and seventh scale steps in minor do not count as chromatic alterations.)

6

TWO VOICES; 2 : 1, 3 : 1, AND 4 : 1; EXERCISES IN ERROR DETECTION

Tell, or write below each example, the errors or weaknesses involved. Use the numbers to refer to specific points.

TWO VOICES; 2 : 1, MAJOR AND MINOR, DIATONIC

Where a sequence occurs in the given voice, use one in the added voice as well.

Where a sequence occurs in the given voice, use one in the added voice as well.

Where eighth notes occur in the C. F., use either a quarter note or two eighths in the added voice.

TWO VOICES; 1 : 1 AND 2 : 1 WITH CHROMATIC ALTERATIONS

Where chromatic inflections occur and at points marked*, imply an altered harmony — in most cases a secondary dominant (dominant embellishing chord).

TWO VOICES; 1 : 1 AND 2 : 1 WITH CHROMATIC ALTERATIONS *(continued)*

④ 1 : 1 or 2 : 1

⑤ 2 : 1

⑥ 2 : 1

TWO VOICES; 2 : 1 (INCLUDING CHROMATIC ALTERATIONS AS DESIRED)

Where eighth notes appear in the C. F., use either a quarter note or two eighths in the added voice.
At fermatas within a chorale melody, the motion may either continue or pause, most often the former.

Chorale Melody: *Ein' feste Burg* (portion)

①

②

Chorale Melody: *Ich steh' an deiner Krippen hier*

TWO VOICES; 3 : 1

(Chromatic alterations may be included as desired, from this point on.)
At places where the C. F. has the triplet rhythm, the added voice may either take over the "1" role
(in the 3 : 1 relationship), or it may continue to move in triplets.

(C minor)

*This C. F. is essentially the same as that used in Exercises 7a and 7b on page 11, and the counterpoint to it here may be an elaboration of the solution there.

Consider the possibility of imitation between the voices.

TWO VOICES; 4 : 1

(Add a voice in sixteenth notes.)

①

Chorale Melody: *Freu' dich sehr, O meine Seele* (first two phrases)

②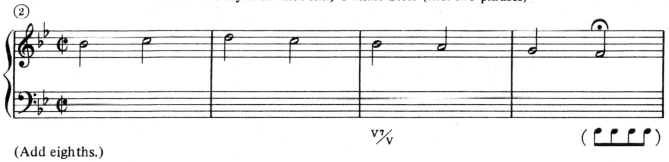

V⁷/V

(♪♪♪♪)

(Add eighths.)

vi
(I⁶)

(♪♪♪♪ ♪)

③

Chorale Melody: *Alle Menschen müssen sterben* (first two phrases)

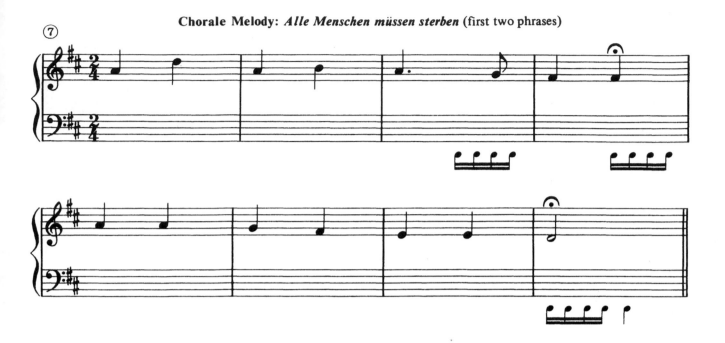

Continue the lower voice, using any values desired, provided an overall rhythm of sixteenth notes is maintained.

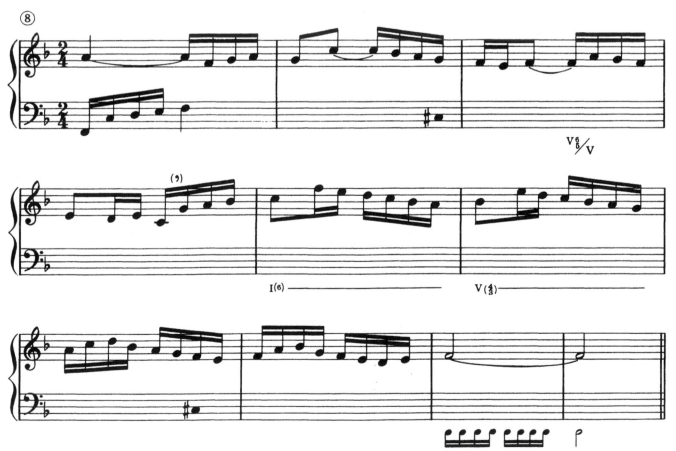

Note: For an additional 4 : 1 exercise, see passacaglia theme no. 6 on page 31.

TWO VOICES; COMPREHENSIVE EXERCISE (1 : 1, 2 : 1, 3 : 1, 4 : 1)

① 1 : 1

② 2 : 1

(G major)

③ 3 : 1

V⁷/ii

④ 4 : 1

TWO VOICES; CONVERSION OF A GIVEN 1 : 1 VERSION TO OTHER RHYTHMS

In ②, convert the 1 : 1 counterpoint given in ① to a version that maintains an eighth-note rhythm, with the motion distributed between the voices as desired. Both voices may occasionally move in eighth notes at the same time. In ③, convert ① to a version using a triplet rhythm, in ④ to one using a sixteenth-note rhythm – with the motion distributed between the voices in each case.

TWO VOICES; CONVERSION OF 1 : 1 TO OTHER RHYTHMS

In ① , write a 1 : 1 counterpoint to the given melody. In ② , convert ① to a version that maintains a quarter-note rhythm, with the motion distributed between the voices as desired. Both voices may occasionally move in quarter notes at the same time. In ③ , convert ① to a version using a quarter-note triplet rhythm, in ④ , to one using an eighth rhythm, with the motion distributed between the voices in each case.

TWO VOICES; FOURTH SPECIES, SUSPENSIONS

A. In ②, convert the 1 : 1 counterpoint given in ① to fourth species by delaying the upper voice by half a beat. In ③, delay the lower voice instead. Where suspensions result, indicate the suspended note with an S, the note of resolution with an R; also add figures (below the staves) to describe the intervals involved in each suspension. If a harmony tone results, indicate that with an H. If the result of shifting a voice is unsatisfactory, mark the beat in question with a U. (This exercise might well be done in class as a demonstration of the fourth species.)

B. By means of a tie or a repeated note, create a suspension in each of the following, in the voice marked X. Write these on the staff below the 1 : 1 versions (① has already been done as an example). Below each suspension add numbers describing it (4 - 3, etc.).

31

TWO VOICES; FOURTH SPECIES, SUSPENSIONS *(continued)*

C. By means of ties or repeated notes, create suspensions in the following passage. Have some in the upper voice, some in the lower. Indicate each suspended note with an S and add numbers to describe each suspension.

D. By means of ties, convert the following passage to fourth-species counterpoint. Where a suspension results, indicate the suspended note with an S and add numbers to describe the suspension.

SUSPENSIONS; EXERCISE IN ERROR DETECTION

E. For each numbered point above the staff, identify the error involved — either orally or on a separate sheet.

33

TWO VOICES; FOURTH SPECIES, SUSPENSIONS *(continued)*

Where suspensions occur in the following passages, indicate the suspended note with an S, the note of resolution with an R; also add figures below the music to describe the intervals involved in each suspension. Be prepared to comment on any delayed or ornamented resolutions.

Fuga Sopra: Magnificat (Organ)

A.

Bach

Man.

Herr Jesu Christ, dich zu uns wend

Telemann

B.

Fugue in D Minor (Organ) from *Messe pour les Paroisses*

C.

Couperin

D. On a separate sheet write a short two-voice passage that contains several suspensions.

TWO-VOICES; REDUCTION OF A FOURTH-SPECIES COMPOSITION TO ITS 1 : 1 BASIS; HARMONIC ANALYSIS

On the blank staves, reduce the upper voice to its basic form — that is, a line as close as possible to the underlying 1 : 1 relationship with the bass. This will mainly involve eliminating nonharmonic tones and shifting notes to their "normal" position. The resulting line will consist mostly of three eighth notes to a measure, although in some cases (measures 4, 6, etc.) rests and some sixteenth notes may be used if desired. When this process has been completed, write a harmonic analysis (chord symbols) below the bass.

Partita No. 6, Corrente

Bach

WRITING OF GROUNDS AND PASSACAGLIAS

Write a short ground or a passacaglia on one of the themes given below, the number of variations to be specified by the instructor. If the assignment is undertaken after the text material through Chapter 6 has been covered, only two voices should be used; if it is to be done after students have progressed through Chapter 14, three (or four) voices may be employed. In any case, Chapter 19 should be read first. In general, the first variation or two should be of relatively moderate rhythmic activity, the succeeding ones progressively more animated. The various species may be used, as well as dotted rhythms, ties, and so forth.

*Counterpoint Example 6 with a lower voice moving consistently in sixteenth notes, as Bach does in Var. 11 of the C minor Passacaglia.

SUITE MOVEMENT (TWO VOICES); ANALYSIS

The instructor should specify which of the following directions apply:
1) add chord symbols;
2) circle nonharmonic tones;
3) label nonharmonic tones;
4) place numbers between the staves to describe the vertical intervals (with numbers for unessential intervals in parentheses);
5) bracket — and label if necessary — any recurring motivic patterns.

French Suite No. 4

Bach

TWO-PART INVENTIONS; STRUCTURAL ANALYSIS

Analyze the following invention, using the same approach as in Example 13, Chapter 10 of the text. Label and bracket each appearance of the motive — and of the countermotive if one is involved. Also indicate episodes, along with the source of their material, and cadences, including the key of each.

Two-Part Invention No. 11

Bach

TWO-PART INVENTIONS; WRITING OF COUNTERPOINTS TO MOTIVES

In each case, continue the top voice to form a counterpoint to the invention motive restated in the bottom voice. If desired, any of the motives given here may be used as the basis for an entire invention or a specified portion of one (for example, the first four announcements plus one episode). In ⑥, space is provided to continue the invention beyond the first two announcements.

TWO-VOICES; COMPLETING OF SEQUENTIAL PATTERNS

Extend each of the following brief passages by means of sequential repetition, up to the point indicated.

THREE VOICES, 1 : 1; EXERCISES IN ERROR DETECTION

Beneath each example list the errors it contains, identifying their position by means of the numbers given above the examples.

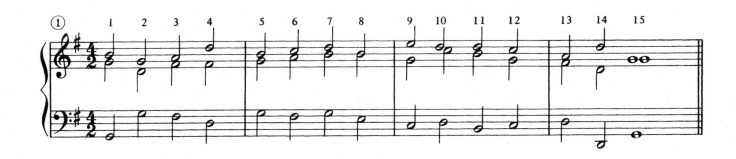

THREE VOICES, 2 : 1; EXERCISE IN ERROR DETECTION

Beneath the example list the errors it contains, identifying their position by means of the numbers given above the example. In the case of errors that occur on the second half of a beat, use the appropriate number followed by the "and" sign (e. g., "9&").

THREE VOICES, 1 : 1 (TOP VOICE GIVEN); CONVERSION TO OTHER RHYTHMS

In ①, add two voices, 1 : 1 (occasional eighth notes may be used). In ②, convert this to a version maintaining an eighth-note rhythm, with the motion distributed among all three voices. (Two voices may sometimes move in eighth-note rhythm at once, rarely all three.) In ③, convert to a version maintaining a triplet rhythm, with the motion distributed.

THREE VOICES, 1 : 1 (BOTTOM VOICE GIVEN); CONVERSION TO OTHER RHYTHMS

In ①, the bottom voice is given; add a middle and a top voice, 1 : 1, both to be written on the upper staff. In ②, convert this to a version maintaining an eighth-note rhythm, with the motion distributed among all three voices as desired. (Two voices may sometimes move in eighth-note rhythm at once, rarely all three.) In ③, convert the 1 : 1 version to one maintaining a triplet rhythm, in ④, to one maintaining a sixteenth-note rhythm, with the motion distributed in each case.

THREE VOICES; SUSPENSIONS

A. Create a suspension in one of the two lower voices in each of the following. Add figures below the lower pair of staves to describe each suspension. (This assignment — as well as B — may profitably be done in class.)

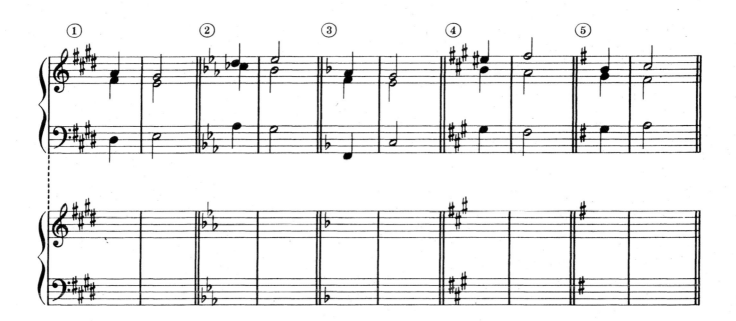

B. Create suspensions (especially the "chain" variety) wherever appropriate in the following.

C. Write a passage in three voices containing several examples of suspension.

THREE VOICES*; SUSPENSIONS (continued)

Indicate each suspended note with an S, each note of resolution with an R. Include harmonic analysis (chord symbols) if the instructor so specifies. These excerpts should also be studied as examples of canonic writing.

*The last example includes a fourth voice near the end.

THREE VOICES, 2 : 1; SUPPLYING A MIDDLE VOICE

A chorale melody and (unfigured) bass are given below. Add a middle voice, which should be written on the treble staff with stems down. For the most part, this voice should move in eighth notes, though it may take longer values when the other voices have eighths. The bass may occasionally be animated to produce an eighth-note rhythm through the addition of notes between the given quarters. (That feature is already present in the original bass, in measures 5, 6, and 10.) The general effect should be one of continuous eighth-note motion, distributed among the voices, though two of them may sometimes move in eighths at the same time. The small notes in the first measure show the beginning of one possible solution; they need not be used if another solution is preferred.

*Die Goldne Sonne, voll Freud und Wonne**(portion)

Bach

*This chorale appears, in the two-voice form shown here, in the Riemenschneider collection of Bach chorale harmonizations. Although no thoroughbass figures are given in this case, the harmonic intent seems quite clear.

THREE VOICES; SUPPLYING A MIDDLE VOICE

Add a middle voice. Have it take the sixteenth-note rhythm when neither of the other voices does. In measures 11 and 12, consider the possibility of imitating the preceding two measures of the top voice.

Organg Sonata No. 3

Bach

THREE-VOICE COMPOSITION: ANALYSIS OPTIONAL ADDING OF FIGURED-BASS SYMBOLS

The instructor should specify which of the following directions apply:
1) add chord symbols;
2) circle nonharmonic tones; indicate each suspended note with an S, each note of resolution with an R;
3) indicate only suspensions, in the way just mentioned, and add figures below the continuo staff to describe the intervals in each. (The figured-bass symbols included in the original have been omitted here.) Be prepared to comment on any delayed or ornamented resolutions.

Sonata da Chiesa a Trē'

Corelli

THREE-VOICES; COMPLETING OF SEQUENTIAL PATTERNS

Extend each of the following patterns by sequential repetition.

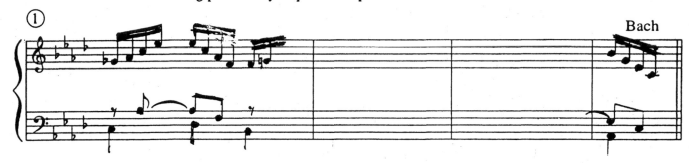

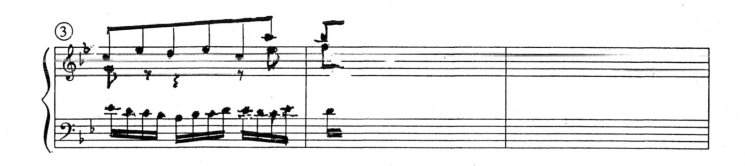

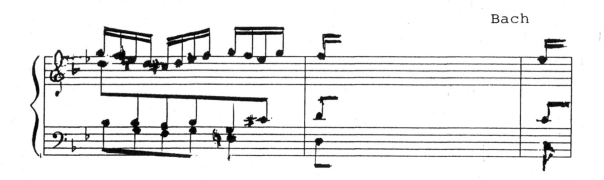

Extend the following pattern by sequential repetition.

In its original form, the six-measure passage shown in Exercise ④ contains two different three-measure sequential patterns; only the first measure of each is shown here. Extend each pattern by sequential repetition. The first will lead naturally into the beginning notes of the second. Note that the basic motion of the first sequence is upward, that of the second, downward.

*The rest and the notes marked with an asterisk do not appear in the sequential repetitions.

IMITATION IN THREE VOICES; WRITING OF ANSWERS, REAL AND TONAL

A. Tell whether each of the following motives or subjects would call for a real or a tonal answer and why.

B. Write an answer below each excerpt. (That placement is only for purposes of comparison; the answer will of course occur — in another voice — *following* the initial statement, and the two will not sound together.) The instructor may wish to defer the actual writing of answers until there has been a chance to analyze a number of works that involve the principles of tonal imitation. The ability to write tonal answers where appropriate will be needed in connection with the work on three-part inventions.

Organ Sonata No. 5, third movement

Sonata No. 3 for Flute and Continuo, Alla Breve

Sonata in G Minor (String Quartet)   *Herr Jesu Christ, dich zu uns wend**

*Chorale preludes for organ.

Lobt Gott, ihr Christen allzugleich*

Buxtehude

Sinfonia No. 9

Bach

Partita No. 5

Bach

Jesus Christus, unser Heiland*

Pachelbel

Gigue

(G minor)

Fugue in F Major (Organ)

Buxtehude

Fugue in C Minor (Organ)

Bach

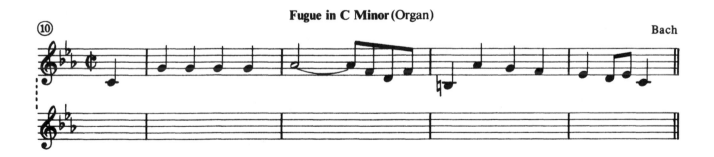

THREE-PART INVENTIONS; STRUCTURAL ANALYSIS

Analyze the following invention, using the same approach as Example 4, Chapter 14 of the text. Label and bracket each appearance of the motive – and of the countermotive if one is involved. Also indicate episodes, along with the source of their material, and cadences, including the key of each.

Sinfonia No. 14

Bach

THREE-PART INVENTIONS; WRITING OF INITIAL ANNOUNCEMENTS

Fill in the missing voices in the following to form the exposition of a three-voice invention in each case. Pitches in small notes are merely suggested; others may be substituted.

*A tonal answer (A, <u>D</u>, C) might well be used here because of the dominant note early in the motive. On the other hand, a real answer could be defended on the grounds that it preserves the triad outline.
The student may choose.

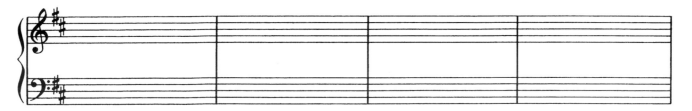

Continuation (beginning of an episode) here if desired.

*Note that the dominant note appears fairly early in the motive and that the motive modulates; plan the answer accordingly.

THREE-VOICE FUGUES; STRUCTURAL ANALYSIS

Analyze the following fugue, using the same approach as in Example 10, Chapter 16 of the text. Label and bracket each appearance of the subject (or answer) and of the countersubject if one is involved. Also indicate episodes, along with the source of their material, and cadences, including the key of each. On a separate sheet, comment on any unusual or significant features.

Well-Tempered Clavier, Book I, Fugue 11

Bach

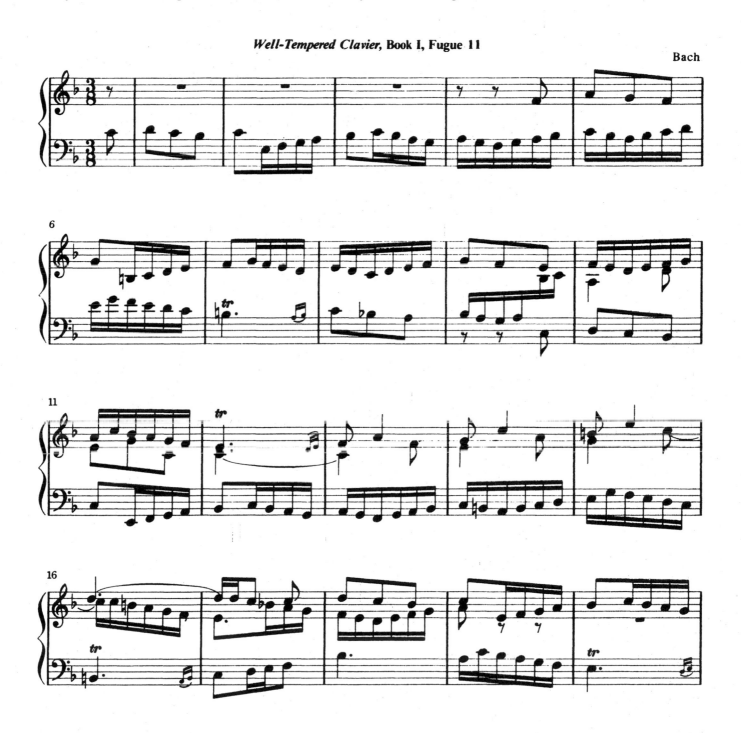

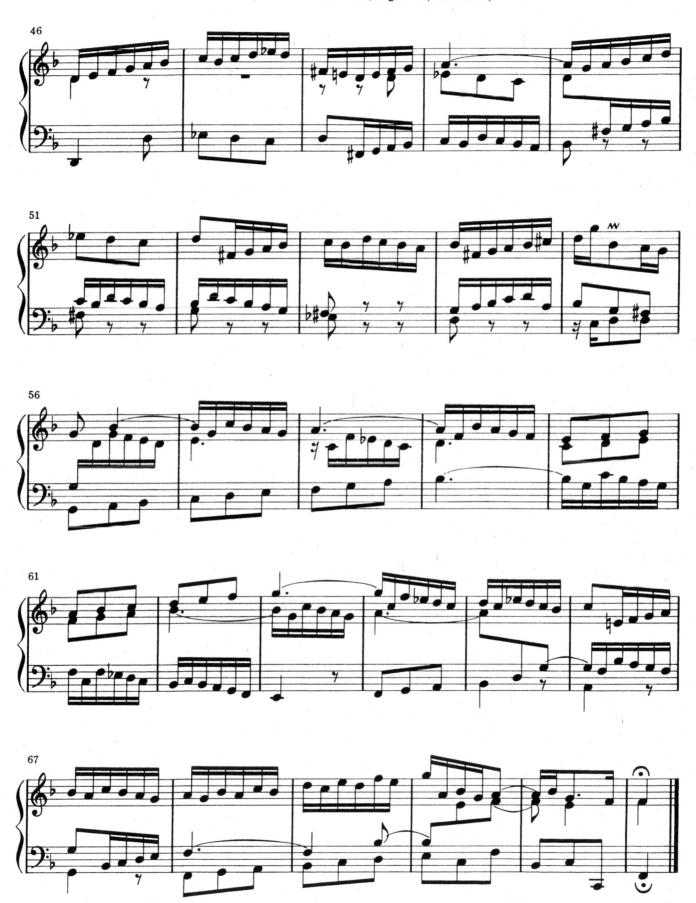

FOUR-VOICE FUGUES; STRUCTURAL ANALYSIS

Analyze the following fugue, using the same approach as in Example 10, Chapter 16 of the text. Label and bracket each appearance of the subject (or answer) and of the countersubject if one is involved. Also indicate episodes, along with the source of their material, and cadences, including the key of each.

Well-Tempered Clavier, Book II, Fugue 7

Bach

WRITING OF STRETTOS

Use each subject as the basis for two two-voice strettos. In ①a and ②a the harmonic interval is to be the octave; the time interval must be determined. In ①b and ②b the first notes of one possible imitation are given — though several others are possible. There is not space here for the second voice to complete the canonic imitation; it will simply stop with the last note of the first voice. Avoid having both voices rest or take long values at the same time; that is, keep the motion going.

*Adapted from *Treatise on the Fugue*, by André Gedalge, Translated and Edited by Ferdinand Davis. Copyright 1965 by the University of Oklahoma Press.

FIVE-VOICE FUGUES; STRUCTURAL ANALYSIS

Analyze the following fugue, using the same approach as in Example 10, Chapter 16 of the text. Since more than one subject is involved here, it is suggested that pencils or pens of different colors be used to bracket the subjects, one color being used consistently for each. This method makes the various elements easily identifiable and is especially helpful at points where subjects are combined.

Well-Tempered Clavier, Book I, Fugue 4

Bach

Note: The exposition of this fugue is analyzed in the text.

In case students do not write their own fugue subjects when they undertake a project in fugue writing, one of the following subjects may be used. The possible presence of elements requiring tonal answers should be carefully considered. Additional fugue subjects are included in the exercises on pages 53, 54, and 55.

CHORALE PRELUDES; ANALYSIS, IDENTIFYING OF TYPES

On a separate sheet, describe briefly the structure of each of the following four excerpts from chorale preludes based on the melody whose first phrase is given at the start. Indicate to what extent each conforms with one of the types discussed in the text. Mention any derivation of accompanying material from the C. F. Include harmonic analysis (beneath the music) if that is requested by the instructor.

CHORALE PRELUDES; STRUCTURAL ANALYSIS

Analyze the following chorale prelude, labeling the various elements on the music itself and adding comments on a separate sheet concerning derivations, relationships between elements, and so forth.

Christ, unser Herr, zum Jordan kam (first two phrases)

Christ unser Herr, zum Jordan kam (Organ Works, Vol. VI, No.18)

Bach

CHORALE PRELUDES; WRITING

The instructor should specify which of the following assignments is to be done:

1. Write a chorale prelude of the "embellished harmonization" type, for organ, based on one of the chorale harmonizations that follow. This will involve adding passing tones, neighbor tones, suspensions, etc., in the various voices, in such a way that a steady rhythmic flow results — normally in eighth-note rhythm, with occasional sixteenths if desired.
2. Write a chorale prelude of the "motivic accompaniment" type. If possible, derive the recurring motivic accompaniment figure from the first phrase of the C. F. The number of voices is optional unless specified by the instructor.
3. Write a chorale prelude of any of the other types discussed in the text.

Nimm von uns, Herr, du treuer Gott

Bach

Das walt' Gott Vater und Gott Sohn

Based on a Bach harmonization*

Liebster Jesu, wir sind hier

Based on a Bach harmonization*

One possible three-voice version of the first two phrases of the above chorale. (Demonstrates the type of exercise called for on page 51 of this Workbook.)

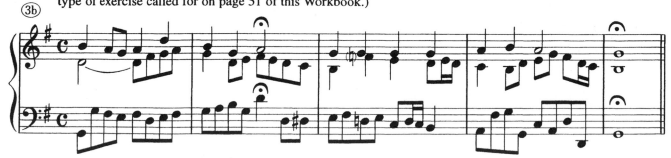

*Some of the nonharmonic tones in the Bach harmonizations have been deleted here in order to allow the student more opportunity for adding these in the process of writing a chorale prelude of the "embellished harmonization" type.

Write a chorale prelude (or a chorale fantasia) based on one of the chorale melodies on this page or the next, or on a chorale melody from another source.

Vater unser im Himmelreich

Vom Himmel hoch, da komm' ich her

O Haupt voll Blut und Wunden

Christ lag in Todesbanden

Jesu, meine Freude

Freu' dich sehr, O meine Seele